I0482140

BIG BREASTS COLORING BOOK

An Erotic Adult Coloring Book

JANE SOLOMON

This page intentionally left blank.

ABOUT THE BOOK

If you're into getting creative and getting in touch with the subject we all love and cherish: beautiful big breasts—this is the book for you. Featuring 8 gorgeous women in luxurious environments with perfect bodies and huge breasts, this book is a must for any breast fanatic.

©Copyright, 2016, by Jane Solomon
All rights reserved.

No part of this book may be reproduced or transmitted in any form or by any means, electronic or
mechanical, including photocopying, recording or by any information storage and retrieval system,
without permission in writing of the copyright owner.

CONTENTS

This page intentionally left blank.

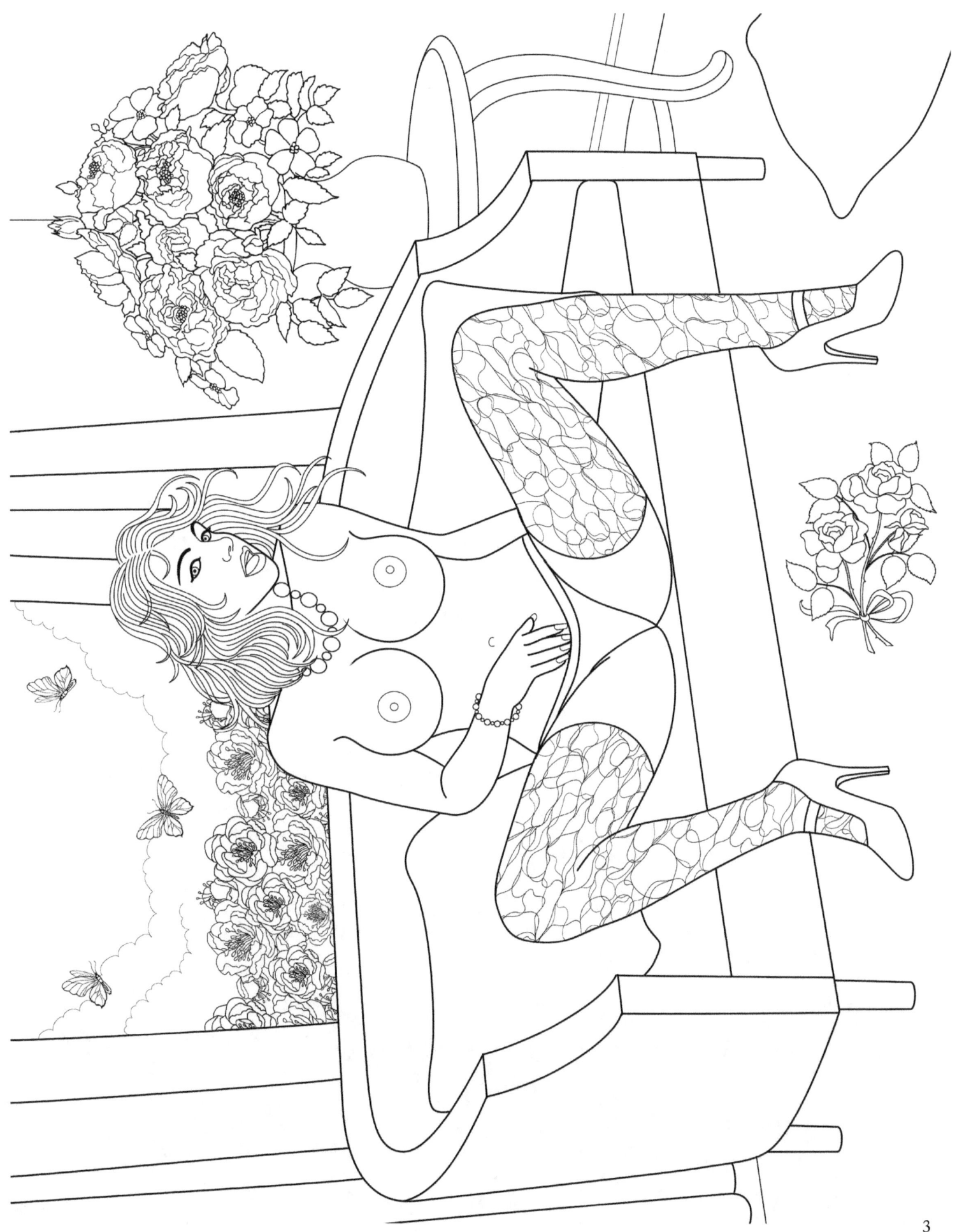

3

Scene 1

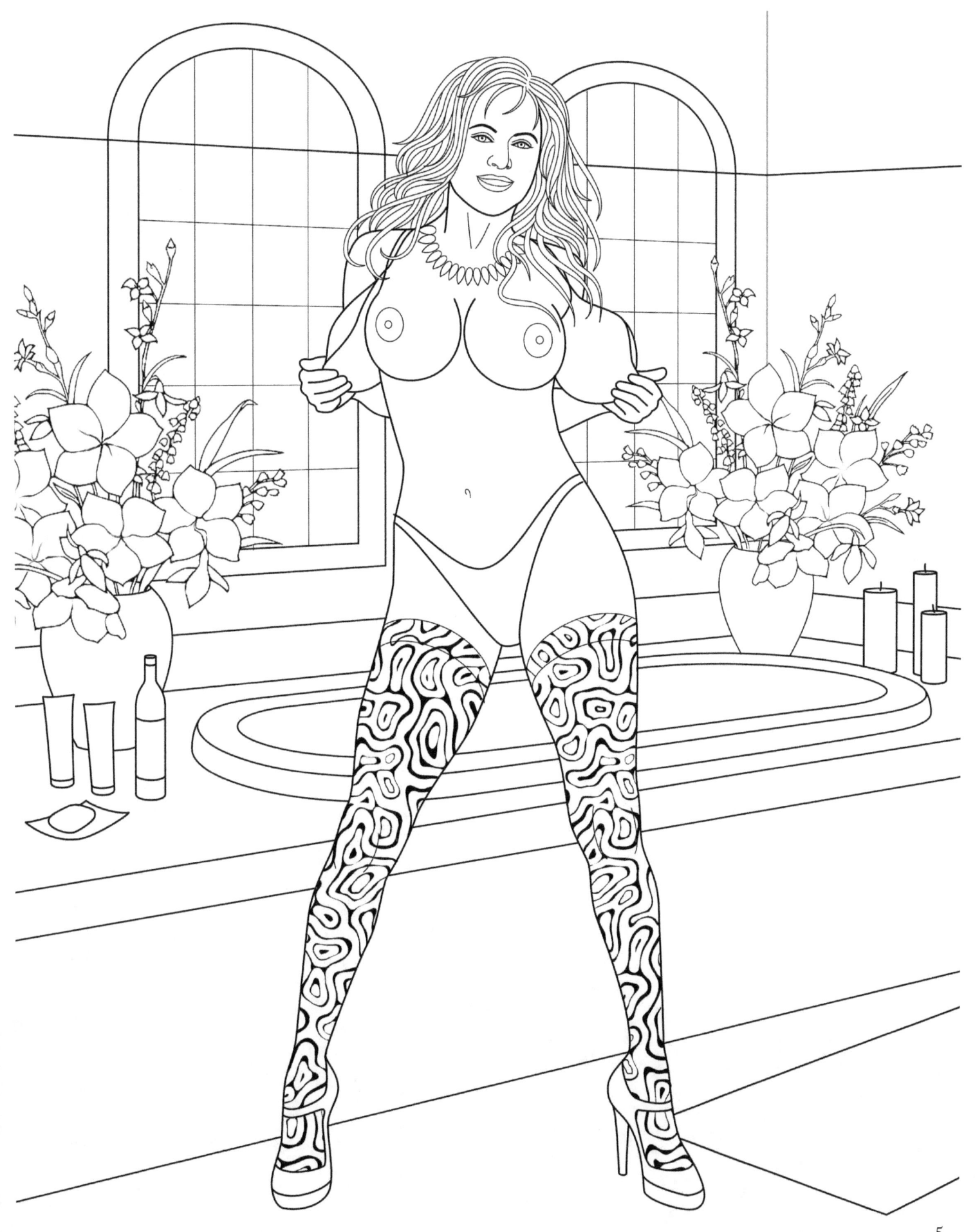

Scene 2

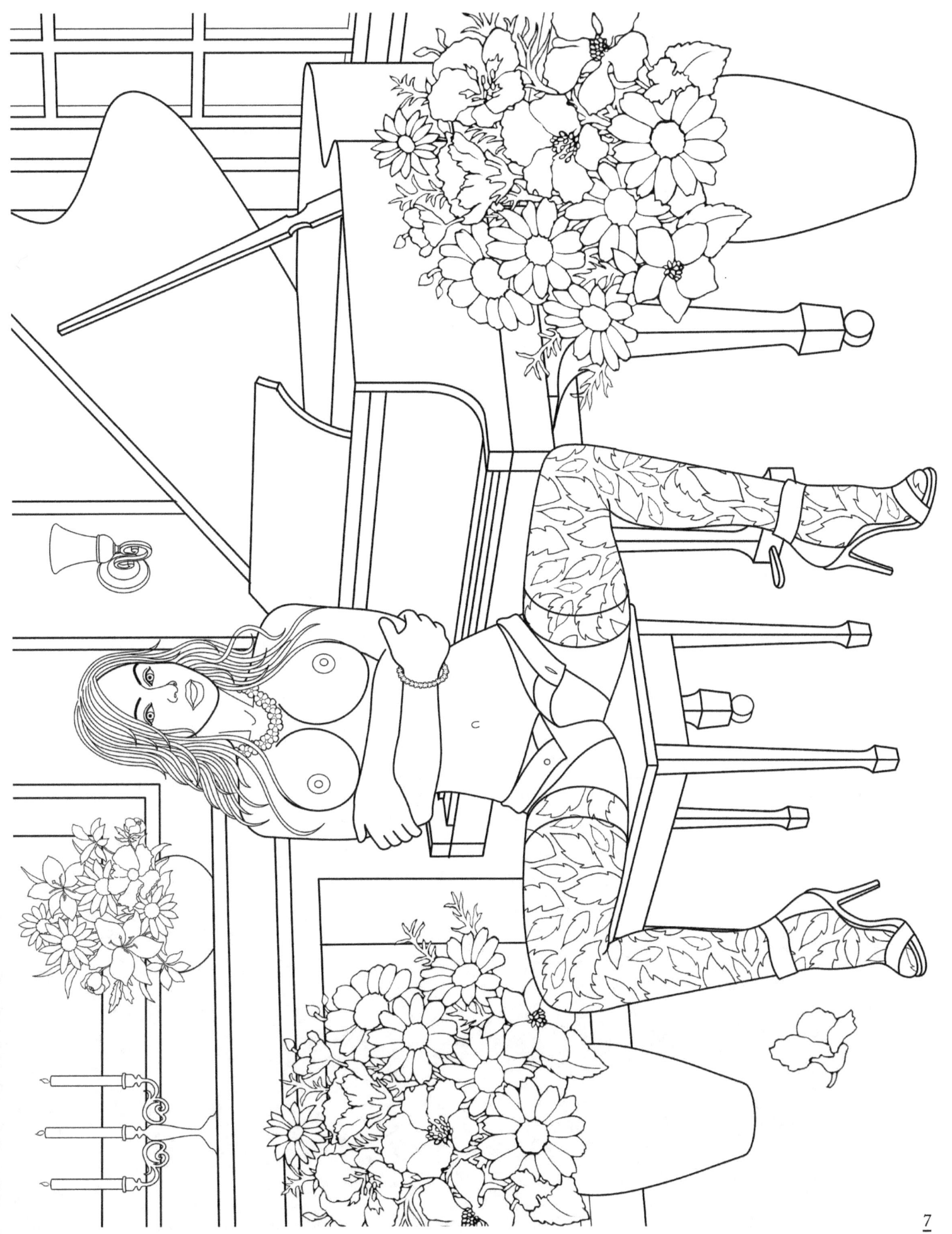

Scene 3

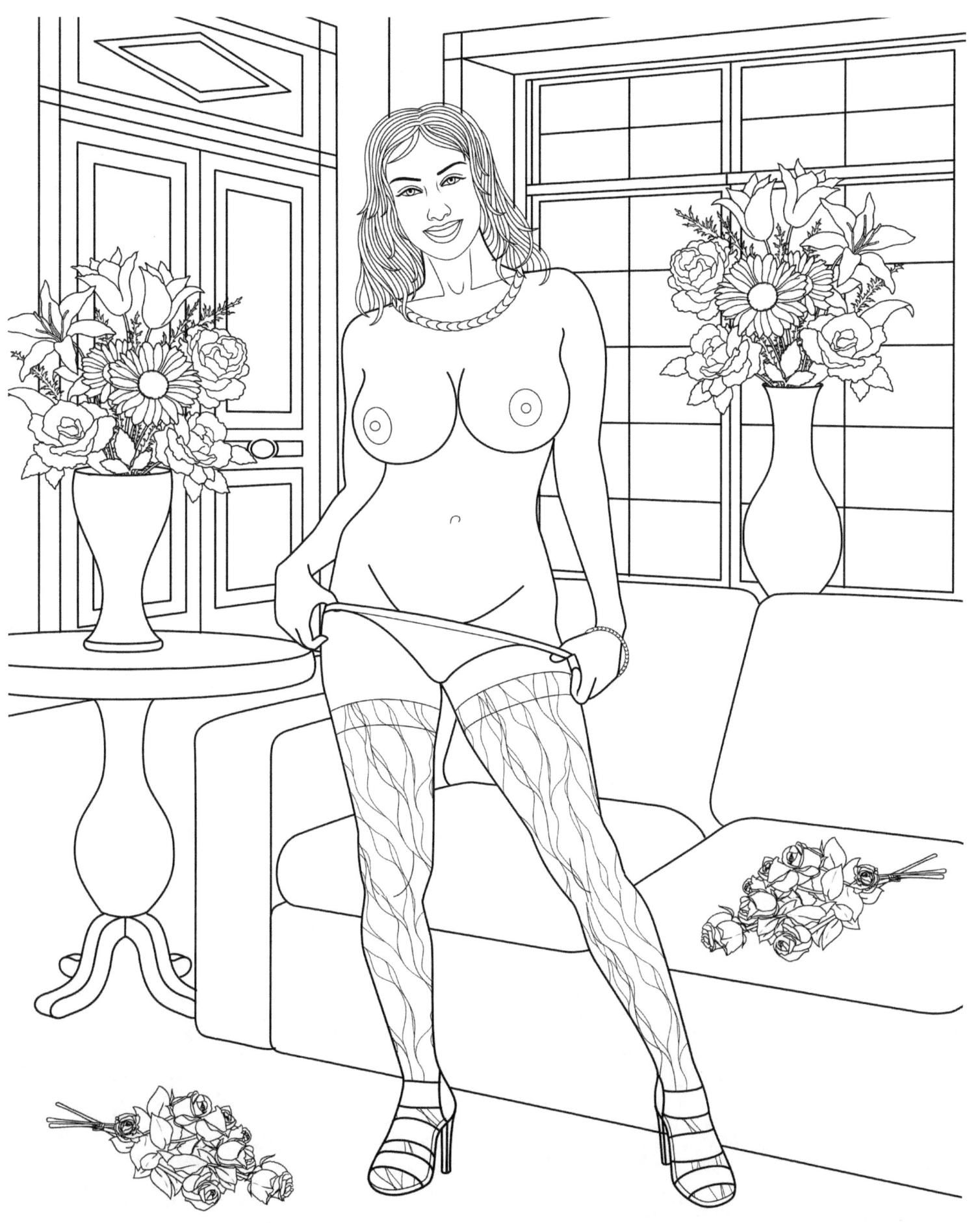

Scene 4

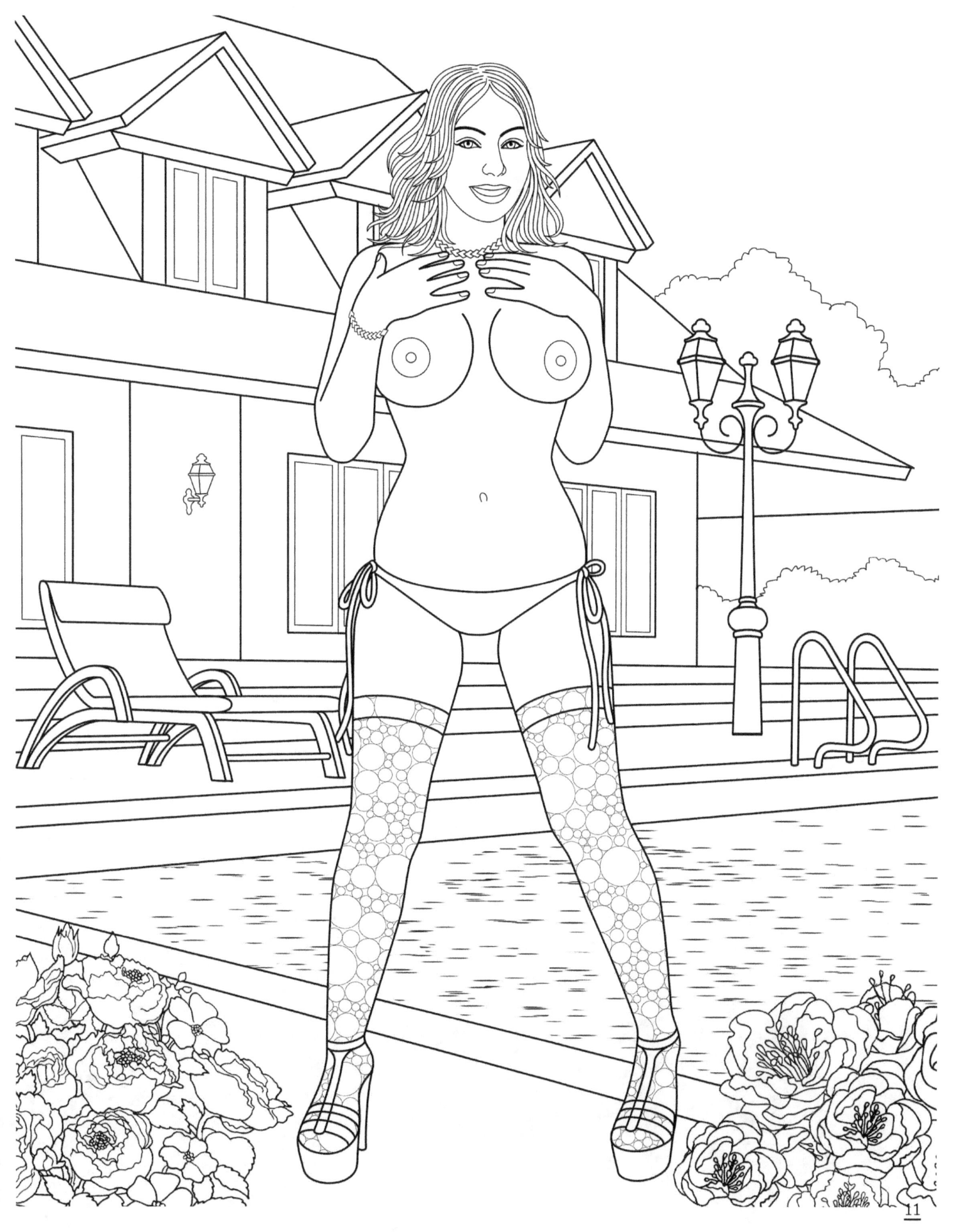

Scene 5

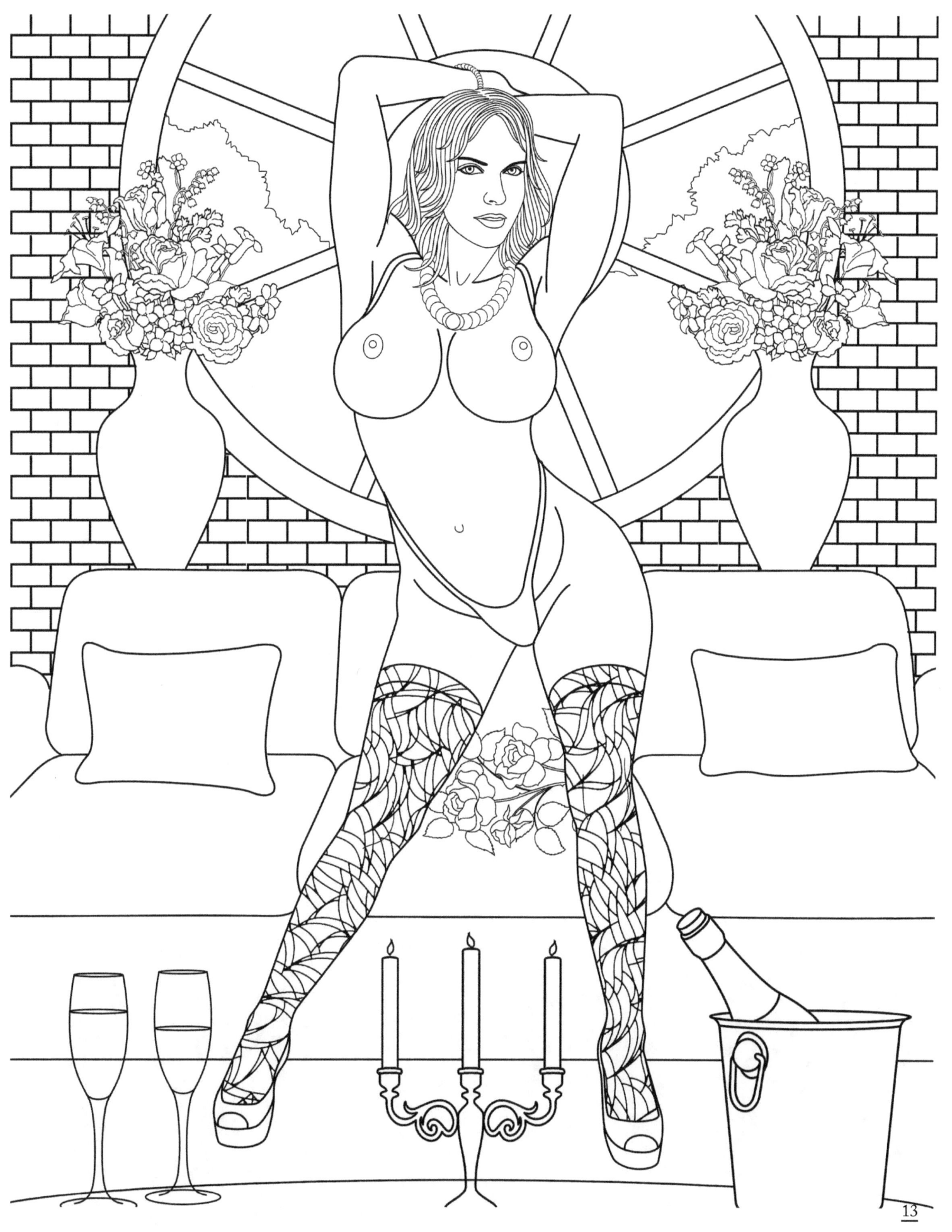

Scene 6

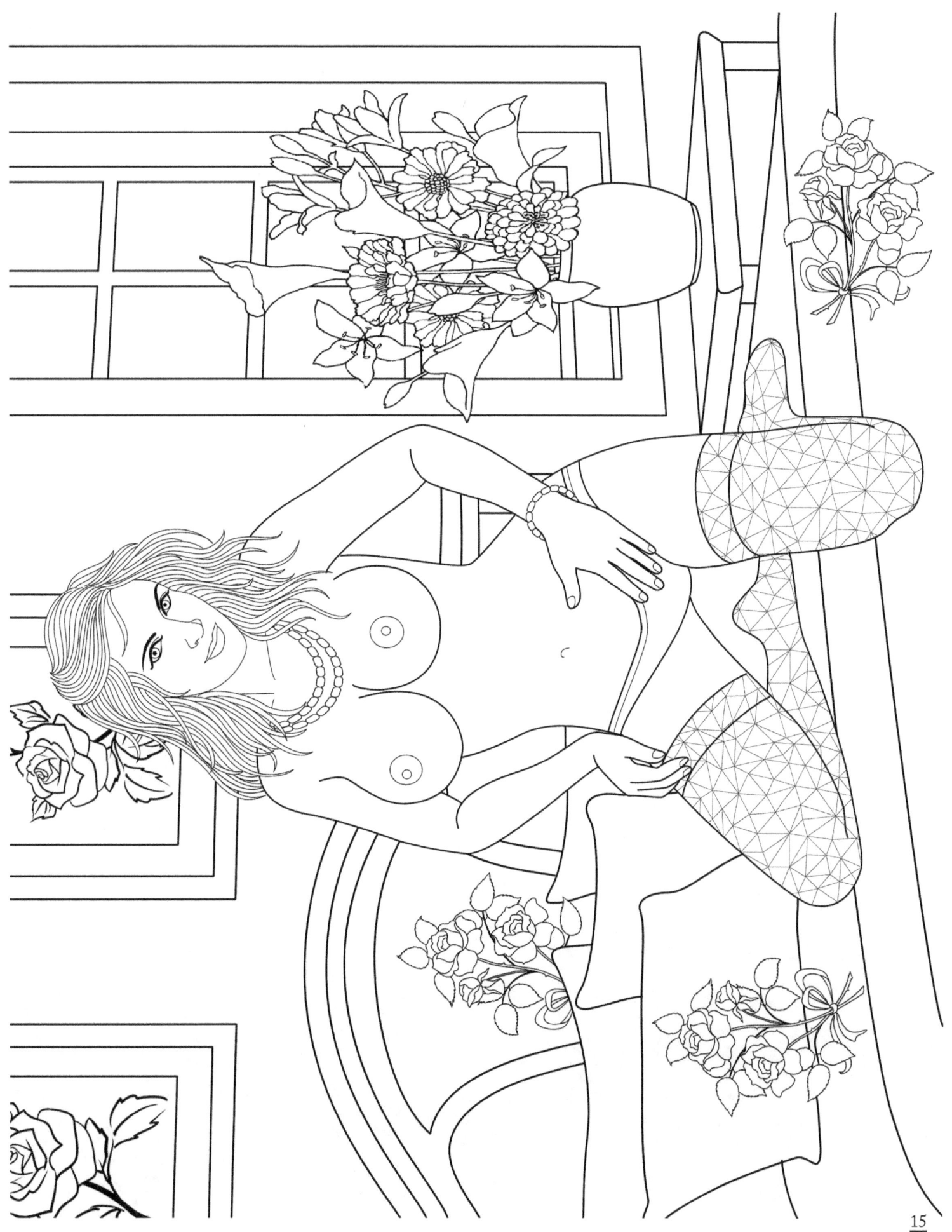

Scene 7

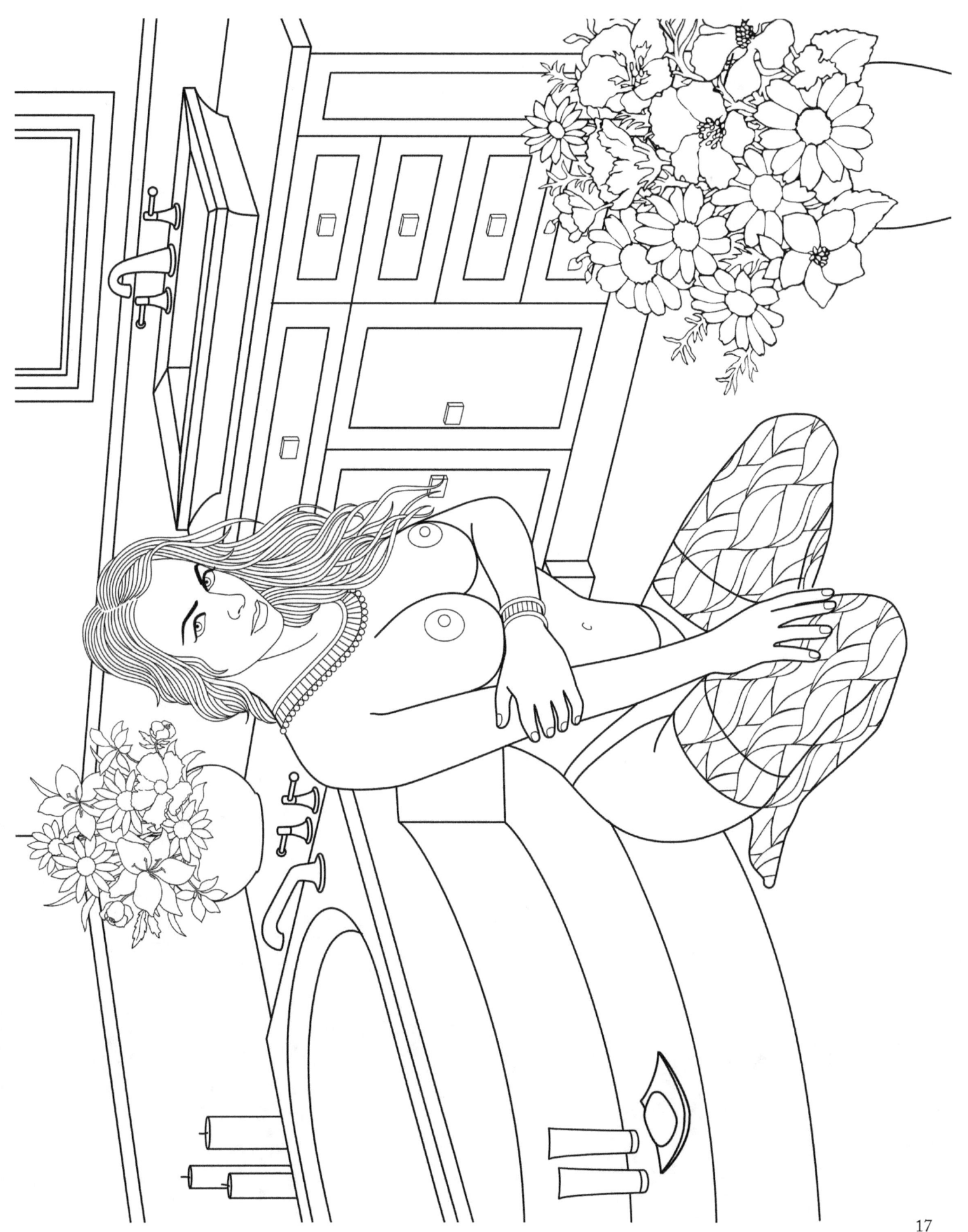

Scene 8

ABOUT THE BOOK

If you're into getting creative and getting in touch with the subject we all love and cherish: beautiful big breasts—this is the book for you. Featuring 8 gorgeous women in luxurious environments with perfect bodies and huge breasts, this book is a must for any breast fanatic.

This page intentionally left blank.

www.ingramcontent.com/pod-product-compliance
Lightning Source LLC
Chambersburg PA
CBHW080534190526
45169CB00008B/3162